ACTIVITY BOOK
Grade 2

Harcourt Brace & Company

Orlando • Atlanta • Austin • Boston • San Francisco • Chicago • Dallas • New York • Toronto • London

http://www.hbschool.com

Copyright © by Harcourt Brace & Company

All rights reserved. No part of this publication may be reproduced or transmitted in any form or by any means, electronic or mechanical, including photocopy, recording, or any information storage and retrieval system, without permission in writing from the publisher.

Permission is hereby granted to individual teachers using the corresponding student's textbook or kit as the major vehicle for regular classroom instruction to photocopy complete pages from this publication in classroom quantities for instructional use and not for resale.

Duplication of this work other than by individual classroom teachers under the conditions specified above requires a license. To order a license to duplicate this work in greater than classroom quantities, contact Customer Service, Harcourt Brace & Company, 6277 Sea Harbor Drive, Orlando, Florida 32887-6777. Telephone: 1-800-225-5425. Fax: 1-800-874-6418 or 407-352-3442.

HARCOURT BRACE and Quill Design is a registered trademark of Harcourt Brace & Company.

Printed in the United States of America

ISBN 0-15-311338-3

2 3 4 5 6 7 8 9 10 129 2000 99

Contents

The Amazing Human Body

Vocabulary Reinforcement: Your Eyes and Ears 1
Critical Thinking: Matching Bones 2
Vocabulary Reinforcement: Working Together 3
Critical Thinking: First Aid for Bleeding 4
Vocabulary Reinforcement: Muscles and Nerves 5

Chapter 1 My Feelings

Critical Thinking: Alike or Different? 6
Reading Skills: Feelings 7
Vocabulary Reinforcement: Words About You 8
Life Skills: Manage Stress 9
Critical Thinking: Showing Respect 10
Vocabulary Reinforcement: Friendly Words 11

Chapter 2 My Family

Vocabulary Reinforcement: Learning and Growing 12
Critical Thinking: Ways We Grow 13
Reading Skills: A Special Visit 14
Critical Thinking: Getting Along 15
Life Skills: Resolve Conflicts 16
Vocabulary Reinforcement: You and Your Family 17

Chapter 3 Caring for My Teeth

Vocabulary Reinforcement: Parts of a Tooth 18
Reading Skills: Tooth Facts 19
Critical Thinking: Brush and Floss 20
Critical Thinking: Eating Right for Healthy Teeth 21
Life Skills: Make Decisions About Your Teeth 22
Vocabulary Reinforcement: Scrambled Words 23

Chapter 4 Keeping Fit and Healthy

Critical Thinking: True or False? 24
Vocabulary Reinforcement: Sunny Day Words 25
Reading Skills: Ben's Busy Day 26
Critical Thinking: Fit and Fun 27

Life Skills: Manage Stress with Exercise **28**
Vocabulary Reinforcement: Fill in for Fitness **29**

Chapter 5 Food for Fitness

Reading Skills: Every Serving Counts **30**
Vocabulary Reinforcement: Fix the Definitions **31**
Critical Thinking: Choose a Healthful Lunch **32**
Vocabulary Reinforcement: Healthful Eating **33**
Life Skills: Make Decisions About Snacks **34**
Critical Thinking: Is It Safe? **35**

Chapter 6 Staying Well

Critical Thinking: Who Is Ill? **36**
Life Skills: Communicate When You Are Ill **37**
Critical Thinking: Will and Phil **38**
Vocabulary Reinforcement: Signs of Illness **39**
Reading Skills: What Do You See? **40**
Vocabulary Reinforcement: Illness Words **41**

Chapter 7 Medicines and Drugs

Reading Skills: Safety with Medicines **42**
Vocabulary Reinforcement: Words About Drugs **43**
Critical Thinking: Don't Chew Tobacco! **44**
Critical Thinking: Make a Better Choice **45**
Vocabulary Reinforcement: Refusing Drugs **46**
Life Skills: Say No to Drugs **47**

Chapter 8 Staying Safe

Critical Thinking: Fire Safety **48**
Life Skills: Resolve Conflicts **49**
Vocabulary Reinforcement: Safety Search **50**
Reading Skills: Betsy's Bike **51**
Critical Thinking: Animal Safety **52**
Vocabulary Reinforcement: Safety Words **53**

Chapter 9 Caring for My Neighborhood

Reading Skills: A Trip to the Hospital **54**
Vocabulary Reinforcement: Hospital Words **55**
Critical Thinking: Recycling **56**
Life Skills: Make Decisions About Trash **57**
Critical Thinking: Facts About Water **58**
Vocabulary Reinforcement: Land, Water, and Air **59**

Name _____ Date _____

Your Eyes and Ears

Vocabulary Reinforcement

1. Label the parts of the eye. Color the iris to match your eyes.

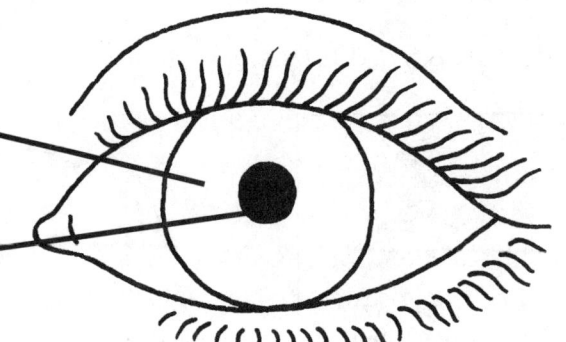

2. Draw something you like to listen to.

The Amazing Human Body
Use with Eyes and Ears.

Name _____ Date _____

Matching Bones

Match the bones to the places where they are found. Draw lines to connect the pictures of bones to the parts of the girl's body.

Critical Thinking

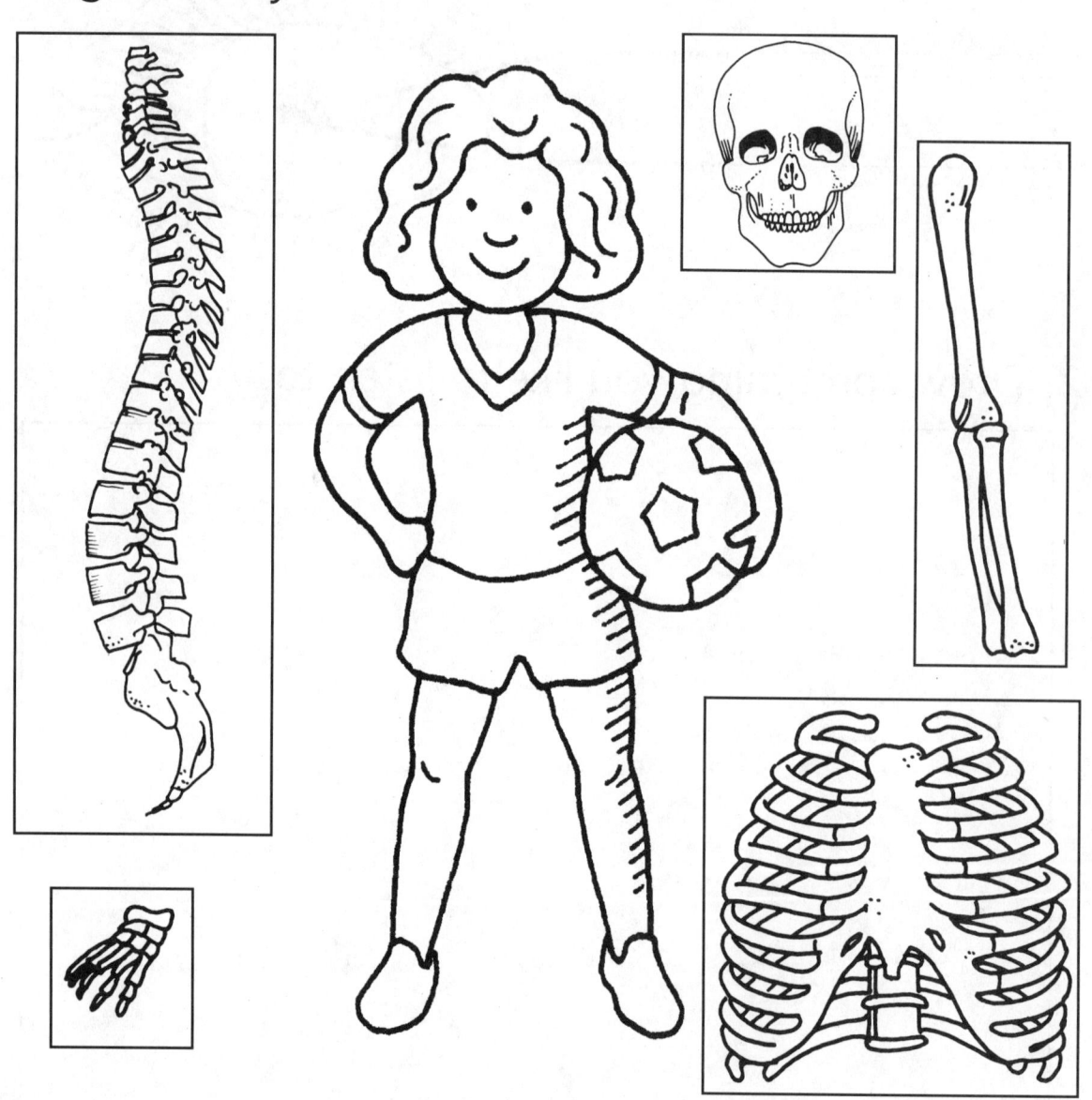

The girl is going to play soccer. Draw something on her that will help protect her leg bones.

Name _____ Date _____

Vocabulary Reinforcement

Working Together

Draw lines to match each part of the digestive system to what it does.

What It Is   **What It Does**

1. mouth   a. chew the food

2. stomach   b. takes food into the body

3. tongue   c. crushes food and turns it into a thick liquid

4. teeth

   d. tastes food and pushes it into the throat

The Amazing Human Body
Use with The Digestive System.

Name _____ Date _____

First Aid for Bleeding

Critical Thinking

Read each of the rules. Circle the letter of the picture that shows how to follow the rule.

1. Use a cloth. Press down right on top of the cut.

a.    b.

2. If the cloth gets too full, do not take it away. Put another cloth on top of it.

a.    b.

3. If you can, raise the bleeding part of the body above the heart.

a.    b.

Remember, never touch another person's blood! Wear gloves if you need to help someone who is bleeding.

Name _____ Date _____

Muscles and Nerves

Vocabulary Reinforcement

Answer each question by writing **muscles** or **nerves**.

1. We need to stretch gently before exercise.

   What are we? _____

2. We tell you about your surroundings.

   What are we? _____

3. We make your muscles work.

   What are we? _____

4. You use us to blink, run, and eat.

   What are we? _____

5. We are connected to the brain.

   What are we? _____

The Amazing Human Body
Use with The Muscular and Nervous Systems.

Name _____ Date _____

Alike or Different?

Critical Thinking

Read each sentence. Decide if it tells a way most children are alike or a way children differ from one another. Draw a line under the correct answer.

1. Children have hair.   alike   different
2. Children are tall.   alike   different
3. Children have eyes.   alike   different
4. Children like purple.   alike   different
5. Children eat food.   alike   different
6. Children have curly hair.   alike   different
7. Children have green eyes.   alike   different
8. Children like broccoli.   alike   different

Name _____ Date _____

Feelings

Reading Skills

Read each story. Look at the faces. Draw a line from each story to the face that matches it.

1. Jason's little brother dropped Jason's crayon box. The crayons are broken.

   a.

2. Jennifer's mother promised to help her make a kite as soon as she had time. "It's time now!" Jennifer's mother says.

   b.

3. Stephanie rides her bicycle every day. One morning she falls off her bike and hurts her knee.

   c.

4. Juan's family moved to a new home. Juan wants to meet new friends. The boy next door asks Juan to play catch.

   d.

Chapter 1 • My Feelings
Use with Lesson 2.

Name _____ Date _____

Vocabulary Reinforcement

Words About You

Write about yourself. Use each of the words in the box in your sentences.

special	different	feelings
worried	afraid	

Choose one of the words from the box. Draw a picture that shows what the word means.

Name _____ Date _____

Manage Stress

Life Skills

Read the story.

> Ted's library book is due today. When he gets to school, Ted remembers that he left the book on the school bus. Ted is worried that he will get into trouble. Ted feels stress.

Draw pictures of two things Ted could do to manage his stress.

Chapter 1 • **My Feelings**
Use with Life Skills: Manage Stress.

Name _____ Date _____

Critical Thinking

Showing Respect

Draw a line under the answer that shows respect.

1. Your sister wants to use your markers.
    a. You tell her to find her own markers.
    b. You share your markers.

2. You spill your friend's milk at lunch.
    a. You say, "I'm sorry."
    b. You tell your friend, "It was your fault."

3. Your grandmother gives you a present.
    a. You say, "Thank you."
    b. You grab the present and ask, "Is that all?"

4. Your brother steps on your toe by mistake.
    a. You hit your brother.
    b. You forgive him when he apologizes.

5. Your dad had to work late.
    a. You offer your dad the last piece of pie.
    b. You whine because he's too tired to take you to a movie.

Name _____ Date _____

Friendly Words

Vocabulary Reinforcement

Fill in the blanks to solve the puzzle.

| polite | friend |
| apologize | respect |

Clues

Down

1. When you say "Please" and "Thank you," you are being ___.
3. Showing ___ means being thoughtful and kind.

Across

2. When you make a mistake, it is good to ___.
4. Someone you like and trust is your ___.

Chapter 1 • My Feelings
Use with Lesson 6.

Name _____   Date _____

Learning and Growing

Vocabulary Reinforcement

Next to each picture, write a word from the box that tells what the picture shows.

> safety
> growing
> senses

1.

2.

3.

12 • Activity Book

Chapter 2 • My Family
Use with Lesson 2.

Name _____ Date _____

Ways We Grow

Critical Thinking

Read the chart. Read the examples below the chart. Put the letter of each example under the correct heading on the chart.

Bodies Growing	Learning Things	Being Responsible

Examples

a. shoes too small

b. can tie shoes

c. clothes too small

d. can read

e. putting away toys

f. can write

g. setting the table

h. baby teeth fall out

i. keeping room neat

Chapter 2 • My Family
Use with Lesson 3.

Name _____ Date _____

A Special Visit

Reading Skills

Read the story. Answer the questions.

   Kim is excited. He is going to meet his grandparents for the first time. They are coming on a plane from Korea. Kim and his little brother Jie helped get the guest room ready. They picked up their toys. They set the table for dinner. Now their home is ready to welcome the grandparents. Kim can hardly wait. He is proud to belong to his family.

1. Why is Kim excited? _____
_____
_____

2. Where are Kim's grandparents coming from?
_____
_____

3. Write one way Kim and Jie helped get their home ready. _____
_____
_____
_____

Name _____ Date _____

Critical Thinking

Getting Along

Circle the letter of the sentence that tells about each picture.

1. a. Family members spend time together.
   b. Family members don't talk to one another.

2. a. Family members make fun of one another.
   b. Family members help one another.

3. a. Family members show love.
   b. Family members hurt one another's feelings.

Name _____ Date _____

Resolve Conflicts

Life Skills

The steps to resolve a conflict are jumbled up. On the lines, write the steps in the correct order. Put a number by each step.

> Agree to disagree.
> Find a way for both sides to win.
> Talk about a solution.
> Stop.

Step ____ _____

Step ____ _____

Step ____ _____

Step ____ _____

16 • Activity Book

Chapter 2 • My Family
Use with Life Skills: Resolve Conflicts.

Name _____ Date _____

Vocabulary Reinforcement

You and Your Family

Use each word in the box in a sentence.

| responsible |
| family |
| chores |
| love |

1. _____

2. _____

3. _____

4. _____

Chapter 2 • **My Family**
Use with Lesson 7.

Name _____ Date _____

Parts of a Tooth

Vocabulary Reinforcement

Look at the diagram of the tooth.
Color each part of the diagram.
Use the right color for each part.

```
roots  = blue
gum    = red
pulp   = green
dentin = orange
enamel = purple
```

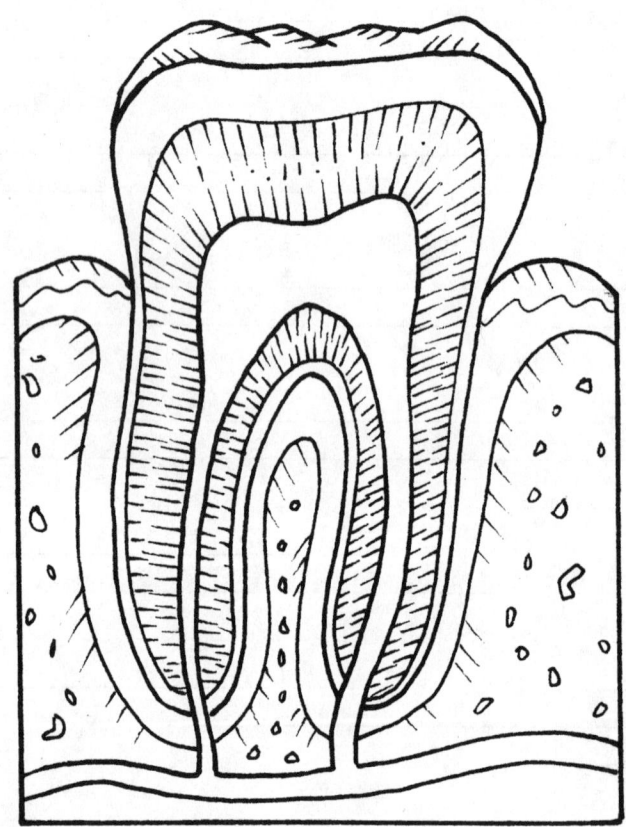

Write the name for the part of the tooth that can

be seen above the gum. _____

18 • Activity Book   Chapter 3 • Caring for My Teeth
                                         Use with Lesson 1.

Name _____ Date _____

Tooth Facts

Read the paragraph.

Reading Skills

> When you were born, you had no teeth showing above the gum. By the time you started kindergarten, you had all 20 primary teeth. You may have started to lose some of these baby teeth when you were in the first grade. Now you have some permanent teeth growing in. By the time you are a young adult, you will have all 32 permanent teeth.

Number the facts in the right order. Put the number 1 by the first thing that happens.

_____ a. You have no teeth showing above the gum.

_____ b. You have some permanent teeth growing in.

_____ c. You have 20 primary teeth.

Chapter 3 • Caring for My Teeth
Use with Lesson 2.

Name _____ Date _____

Brush and Floss

Draw a line under **Yes** if the sentence is true. Draw a line under **No** if the sentence is not true.

Critical Thinking

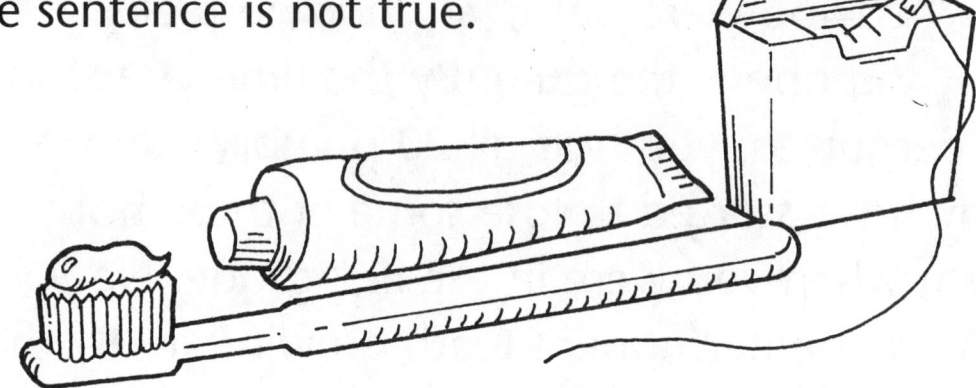

1. Brush the tops of your teeth first.   Yes   No

2. Use a lot of toothpaste when you brush.   Yes   No

3. Use a toothbrush that is the right size for your mouth.   Yes   No

4. Bedtime is the best time to use floss.   Yes   No

5. Press down hard on your toothbrush and move it back and forth.   Yes   No

6. Tooth care products should have the ADA seal on the package.   Yes   No

Name _____ Date _____

Eating Right for Healthy Teeth

Critical Thinking

Look at the pictures. Draw a circle around each food that has calcium. Draw a line under each vegetable snack. Draw an X over each food that has a lot of sugar.

a.
b.
c.
d.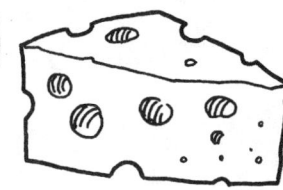

e.
f.
g.
h.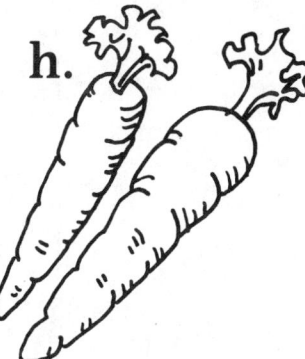

i.
j.
k.
l.

Chapter 3 • Caring for My Teeth
Use with Lesson 4.

Name _____ Date _____

Make Decisions About Your Teeth

Life Skills

Put together a healthy tooth. In each puzzle piece, write or draw a good choice you can make to keep your teeth healthy.

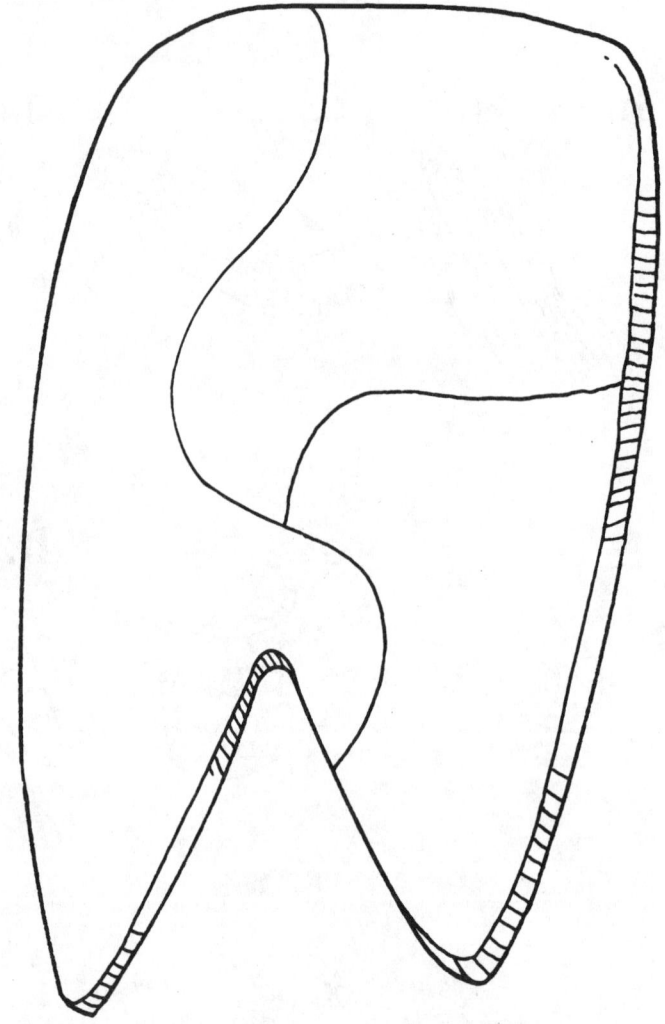

22 • Activity Book

Chapter 3 • Caring for My Teeth
Use with Life Skills: Make Decisions.

Name _____ Date _____

Vocabulary Reinforcement

Scrambled Words

Unscramble the letters to spell the correct words. The clues will help you.

1. losfs ___ ___ ___ ___ ___

   Clue: special thread for cleaning between teeth

2. lacmuic ___ ___ ___ ___ ___ ___ ___

   Clue: something that makes your teeth grow strong

3. iparymr ___ ___ ___ ___ ___ ___ ___

   Clue: your first set of teeth

4. vatyic ___ ___ ___ ___ ___ ___

   Clue: a hole in a tooth

5. rapnetemn ___ ___ ___ ___ ___ ___ ___ ___ ___

   Clue: your second set of teeth

Chapter 3 • Caring for My Teeth
Use with Lesson 5.

Name _____ Date _____

Critical Thinking

True or False?

Circle the **T** if the sentence is true.
Circle the **F** if the sentence is false.

1. Using antibacterial soap helps fight germs. T F

2. You should wash your hands before you touch an animal. T F

3. You should wash your hands after you sneeze. T F

4. Germs are easy to see. T F

5. Fingernails do not need to be cleaned or trimmed. T F

6. Choose one false sentence. Rewrite it to make it true.

_____
_____
_____
_____
_____

Sunny Day Words

Vocabulary Reinforcement

1. Fill in the missing letters.

If you don't wear  __ __ __ __ __ __ ,

you may get a  __ __ __ __ __ .

2. In the center circle of the sun, draw one other way to protect your skin from the sun's rays.

Chapter 4 • Keeping Fit and Healthy
Use with Lesson 2.

Name _____ Date _____

Ben's Busy Day

Finish numbering the pictures in each row to put them in the right order.

Reading Skills

In the Morning

a. _____   b. _____   c. __2__

During the Day

a. _____   b. _____   c. __1__

At Bedtime

  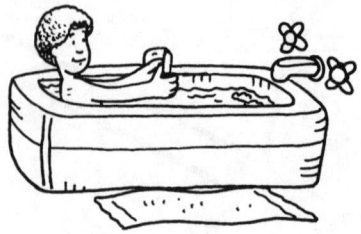

a. _____   b. _____   c. __1__

26 • Activity Book   Chapter 4 • Keeping Fit and Healthy
Use with Lesson 3.

Name _____ Date _____

Fit and Fun

Critical Thinking

● List three things you like to do that are exercise.

_____
_____
_____
_____
_____
_____

● List three things you like to do that are not exercise.

_____
_____
_____
_____
_____
_____

●

Chapter 4 • Keeping Fit and Healthy
Use with Lesson 5.

Name _____ Date _____

Manage Stress with Exercise

Life Skills

Draw a line to connect each step with the right number.

Numbers   **Steps**

Step 1   a. Take one step at a time.

Step 2   b. Think about ways to handle stress.

Step 3
                     c. Learn ways to relax.
Step 4
                     d. Know how stress feels.

Draw a favorite way to manage stress.

[ ]

Name _____ Date _____

Fill In for Fitness

Vocabulary Reinforcement

Write the correct words from the box to finish the sentences.

germs
sunburn
sunscreen
exercise
fit

1. Washing with soap and water _____ helps kill _____ .

2. The sun's rays can give you a _____ in any weather.

3. Make your heart, lungs, and muscles strong _____ with _____ .

4. Protect your skin by wearing _____ when you go outside.

5. Getting lots of exercise and sleep helps keep you healthy and _____ .

Chapter 4 • Keeping Fit and Healthy
Use with Lesson 7.

Name _____ Date _____

Every Serving Counts [Reading Skills]

Molly made a list of everything she ate yesterday. Put the number of the correct food group next to each thing on the list. Use the numbers from the box.

Food Groups	
1 = fats, oils, sweets	2 = milk, yogurt, cheese
3 = meat, poultry, fish, dried beans, eggs, nuts	4 = vegetables
5 = fruits	6 = bread, cereal, rice, pasta

Molly's List

a. glass of milk _____

b. 2 slices of toast _____

c. 1 egg _____

d. orange sections _____

e. apple juice _____

f. carrot sticks _____

g. sandwich (chicken, 2 slices rye bread) _____ _____

h. cookies _____

i. green beans _____

j. rice _____

k. baked fish _____

l. salad _____

Name _____ Date _____

Fix the Definitions

Vocabulary Reinforcement

The definitions below have some extra words that change the meaning of the term. Draw a line through the extra words to make the definitions correct.

1. Food Guide Pyramid

   a round chart that shows which foods you should not eat

2. wastes

   materials the body does not need very often

3. energy

   the power from batteries your body needs to do some things

4. serving

   the amount of a cooked food a person eats at one breakfast time

Chapter 5 • Food for Fitness
Use with Lesson 3.

Name _____ Date _____

Choose a Healthful Lunch

Critical Thinking

You and your friends go to a diner for lunch. Look at the menu. Choose something from each section. Circle your choices. Try to choose a healthful lunch.

Soups
chicken and rice
tomato
vegetable chili

Drinks
caffeine-free cola
lemonade
milk
orange juice
apple juice

Desserts
frozen yogurt
hot fudge sundae
strawberries
frozen juice bar
oatmeal raisin cookies

Sandwiches
tuna salad
grilled cheese
fried fish
turkey
hot dog
veggie burger

Extras
fries
chips and dip
applesauce
cole slaw
carrots and celery
green salad

Name _____ Date _____

Healthful Eating

Vocabulary Reinforcement

Each list is missing a word. Write a word from the box on the line to finish each list.

| fat | lunch | Ingredients |

List 1

Things to Stay Away From

sweets

very salty foods _____

foods with a lot of _____

List 2

_____ in Peanut Butter

roasted peanuts

vegetable oil

salt

List 3

Kinds of Meals

dinner

_____

breakfast

Chapter 5 • Food for Fitness
Use with Lesson 5.

Name _____ Date _____

Life Skills

Make Decisions About Snacks

Under each picture, write the first letter of the word the picture shows.

1. ___ ___ ___ ___ ___ ___

2. ___ ___ ___ ___ ___ ___ ___

3. ___ ___ ___ ___ ___ ___

Read the letters in each line to find a good decision you can make about food.

Name _____ Date _____

Is It Safe?

Critical Thinking

Draw a line under the best choice.

1. Jacob's cat took a bite of Jacob's tuna sandwich.

    a. Jacob should keep eating the sandwich.

    b. Jacob should stop eating the sandwich. He should find something else to eat.

2. Annie is at soccer practice. She is thirsty. Lisa says Annie can drink from her water bottle.

    a. Annie should get her own drink.

    b. Annie should drink from Lisa's water bottle.

3. Sam's mother lets him help stir the cookie dough. The dough has raw eggs in it. Sam's sister wants to taste the dough.

    a. Sam should tell his sister to wait until the cookies are baked.

    b. Sam should give his sister a bite of raw cookie dough.

4. Julie finds a candy bar on the playground. The wrapper is a little dirty, but it isn't torn. The candy bar is Julie's favorite kind.

    a. Julie should eat the candy bar.

    b. Julie should not eat or even touch food she finds on the ground.

Chapter 5 • Food for Fitness
Use with Lesson 7.

Name _____ Date _____

Who Is Ill?

Critical Thinking

Circle the letters of the pictures that show children who are ill.

a.

b.

c.

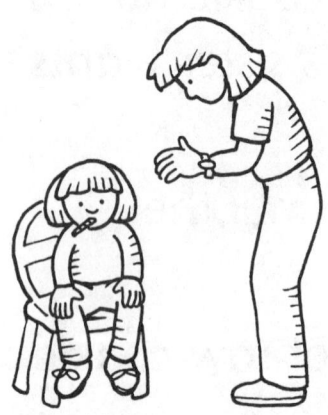
d.

e.

f.

36 • Activity Book

Chapter 6 • **Staying Well**
Use with Lesson 1.

Name _____ Date _____

Communicate When You Are Ill

Life Skills

You need to know what to say when you tell someone you are ill. Match the feelings with the words. Draw lines to connect each way you feel with the right words to say.

How You Feel

1. hot and weak
2. pain or pressure in your head
3. like throwing up
4. like the room is spinning
5. hurts when you swallow

What to Say

a. "I am sick to my stomach."
b. "I have a fever."
c. "I have a sore throat."
d. "I am dizzy."
e. "I have a headache."

Chapter 6 • Staying Well
Use with Life Skills: Communicate

Name _____ Date _____

Will and Phil

Critical Thinking

Will and Phil are twins. They look alike, but they act differently. Will takes care of himself. He tries not to spread germs. Phil doesn't take care. He spreads germs. You can tell the twins apart by how they act. Write Will or Phil under each picture.

1. _____

2. _____

3. _____

4. _____

38 • Activity Book

Chapter 6 • Staying Well
Use with Lesson 2.

Name _____ Date _____

Signs of Illness

Vocabulary Reinforcement

Finish the story. Fill in the blanks with the right words. Use the words from the box.

| disease | scabs | ill | pox |
| sneezing | germs | cold | |

Two children are absent from the second grade class. They are both _____. Sean is coughing, sniffling, and _____. He has a _____. Gina had itchy bumps on her skin. They turned into blisters and _____. Gina has chicken _____. Each child has a _____ that can be spread by _____.

Chapter 6 • Staying Well
Use with Lesson 3.

Name _____ Date _____

What Do You See?

Reading Skills

Write the best title for each picture story.
Choose a title from the box.

| Allergy   Asthma |

1. Title _____

2. Title _____

40 • Activity Book

Chapter 6 • **Staying Well**
Use with Lesson 5.

Name _____ Date _____

Illness Words

Vocabulary Reinforcement

Fill in the blanks to solve the puzzle.

Clues

Across

1. illness caused by a reaction in the body
3. tiny bugs that lay eggs in hair
4. shots or pills to keep people from getting some diseases

Down

1. an illness that makes it hard to breathe
2. another name for illness
5. not well

Chapter 6 • Staying Well
Use with Lesson 6.

Activity Book

Name _____ Date _____

Safety with Medicines

Reading Skills

Read each story. Then circle the right letter to answer the question.

> Aunt Luisa put the medicine away. She put it in the top cabinet. No children can reach the medicine.

1. What is the story about?

  a. Aunt Luisa can reach high places.

  b. Aunt Luisa put the medicine in a safe place.

> Father is helping Kaleel take medicine. "Hurry up," Kaleel says. "Just give me one spoonful." Father says, "Wait, Kaleel. I need to read the instructions."

2. Why does Kaleel's father want to wait?

  a. He wants to give Kaleel the right amount of medicine.

  b. He doesn't want Kaleel to feel better.

> Nan was on a field trip with her class. Her head started to hurt. Nan's teacher said, "I will call your mother to find out if you can take some medicine."

3. Why did the teacher want to call Nan's mother?

  a. She didn't believe Nan was ill.

  b. She knew children should not take medicines without a family member's permission.

Name _____ Date _____

Words About Drugs

Vocabulary Reinforcement

Finish the sentences. Choose a word from the box to write on each line.

> medicines
> caffeine
> drugs
> instructions

1. Some soft drinks have a drug called _____ .

2. When you must take medicine, it is important that an adult read the _____ on the label.

3. Not all drugs are _____, but all _____ are drugs. (Hint! Use the same word two times.)

4. Caffeine and other _____ affect children more than adults, because children have smaller bodies.

Chapter 7 • Medicines and Drugs
Use with Lesson 4.

Name _____ Date _____

Don't Chew Tobacco!

Critical Thinking

> Some tobacco is made to chew. Chewing tobacco contains nicotine, like other kinds of tobacco. Even though it is not smoked, chewing tobacco hurts the body.

Follow the directions to show how chewing tobacco hurts the body.

1. Juice from chewing tobacco hurts the gums. Color the gums red.
2. Chewing tobacco can make the teeth loose. Color the teeth blue.
3. Chewing tobacco can cause cancer of the lips and tongue. Color the lips and tongue purple.
4. All tobacco causes bad breath. Use green to show bad breath.

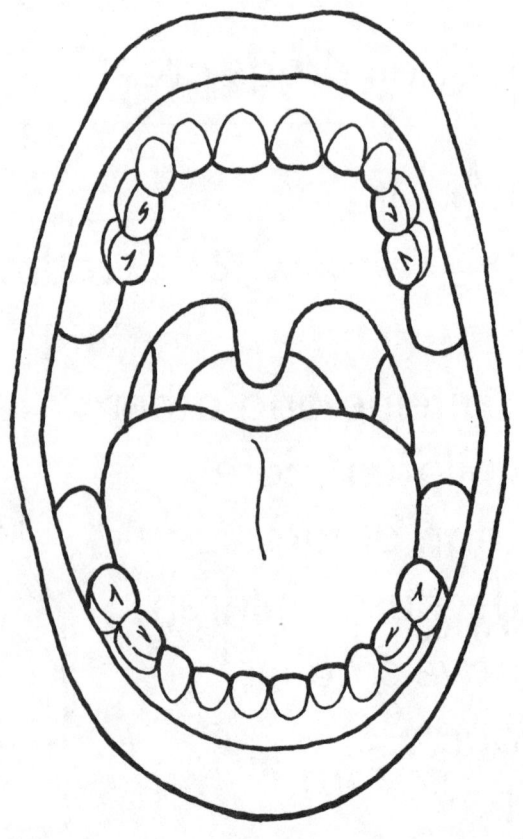

44 • Activity Book

Chapter 7 • Medicines and Drugs
Use with Lesson 5.

Name _____ Date _____

Make a Better Choice

Critical Thinking

Draw a line under the best choice.

1. Hannah is thirsty. The only drink she can find in the refrigerator is beer.

   a. Hannah drinks a little beer.

   b. Hannah drinks water.

2. Devon's mom made a dessert with alcohol in it. The dessert is for adults, but Devon wants to sneak a taste.

   a. Devon eats an apple instead.

   b. Devon decides that a little taste of the dessert won't hurt him.

3. Michael is skateboarding with some older boys. The older boys are drinking beer. They want Michael to try a dangerous jump.

   a. Michael tries the jump.

   b. Michael decides to find another group to skate with.

4. Mei's friend Shawna dares Mei to drink a glass of wine.

   a. Mei drinks the wine so Shawna won't think she's a baby.

   b. Mei refuses. She goes home and tells her mom.

Chapter 7 • Medicines and Drugs
Use with Lesson 6.

Name _____ Date _____

Refusing Drugs

Vocabulary Reinforcement

Fill in the squares. Use the clues for help. When you are finished, read the words going down for an important message.

1. ☐☐☐e☐
2. ☐☐☐☐
   a
   f
   e
3. s
   ☐☐☐☐☐☐
   y
4. ☐☐☐☐☐☐☐
   o
5. ☐☐☐☐☐☐
   o
6. d
   ☐☐☐☐☐
   u
   g
   s

Clues

1. something people do over and over
2. what comes from burning tobacco
3. the drug in beer and wine
4. the drug in tobacco
5. what cigarettes are made from
6. a word that means "say no"

46 • Activity Book   Chapter 7 • Medicines and Drugs
                                  Use with Lesson 7.

Name _____ Date _____

Say No to Drugs

Life Skills

Read the list of reasons to say no to alcohol. Choose three reasons why you would refuse alcohol. Write the letters of the reasons in the drops. On the bottle, write one more reason in your own words.

Reasons to Refuse Alcohol

a. Alcohol is a drug.
b. Alcohol tastes bad.
c. Alcohol is illegal for children.
d. Alcohol can harm the heart.
e. Alcohol is expensive.

Chapter 7 • Medicines and Drugs
Use with Life Skills: Say No.

Name _____ Date _____

Fire Safety

Critical Thinking

The fire safety rules listed below are not correct. There is one wrong word in each rule. Circle the wrong word. Write the correct word on the line.

1. Know all the windows, or ways to get out _____

of your home. _____

2. Try to find at least five ways to leave every room.
_____
_____

3. Pick a place for everyone to meet before leaving _____

your home. _____

4. Call for help from a phone inside your home.
_____
_____

5. If your clothes catch on fire, you should run, _____

drop, and roll. _____

Name _____ Date _____

Resolve Conflicts

Life Skills

Tawny and Keith both want to be in charge of their class project team. They argue all the time, and the team can't get any work done. Help Tawny and Keith resolve their conflict. In the boxes, draw or write what they should do for each step.

1. Agree that there is a problem.

2. Listen to each other.

3. Think of ways to work together.

4. Make the best choice.

Chapter 8 • Staying Safe
Use with Life Skills: Resolve Conflicts.

Name _____ Date _____

Safety Search

Vocabulary Reinforcement

Use the clues to find five vocabulary terms hidden in the puzzle. All the hidden words are printed across. When you find each term, color in the boxes of its letters.

Clues

- a marked place to cross a street safely
- someone you do not know
- a way to practice getting out of a building safely in case of fire
- laws or directions to follow
- a footbridge over a street or highway

f	i	r	e	d	r	i	l	l	y	o
u	s	s	t	r	a	n	g	e	r	h
o	v	e	r	p	a	s	s	o	u	l
d	c	a	l	l	r	u	l	e	s	9
1	1	c	r	o	s	s	w	a	l	k

Now copy the letters and numbers that are left, in order, into the boxes below to answer the question.

What should you do in an emergency?

☐☐☐ ☐☐☐☐☐☐ ☐☐☐☐ ☐☐☐

Name _____ Date _____

Betsy's Bike

Read the story. Then answer the questions.

Reading Skills

> Betsy got a new bike for her birthday. "I want to ride it now!" she said. "Not yet," said Betsy's dad. "We have to get you a new helmet first." Betsy and her dad went to the bike store. Betsy's dad made sure the helmet fit Betsy right. "No riding without a helmet!" he told her. Betsy promised. While they were at the store, dad got Betsy a light for her bike.

1. When did Betsy get her new bike? _____
_____

2. What did Betsy have to get before she could ride her bike? _____
_____

3. What did Betsy promise? _____
_____

4. What else did Betsy's dad buy at the store? _____
_____

Chapter 8 • Staying Safe
Use with Lesson 6.

Name _____ Date _____

Animal Safety

Match the pictures to the rules the children are breaking. Draw a line to connect each picture with the correct rule.

Critical Thinking

1.

2.

3.

4.

Rules

a. Never bother an animal when it is eating.

b. Never touch a wild animal.

c. Don't make loud noises around an animal.

d. Never tease an animal.

52 • Activity Book

Chapter 8 • Staying Safe
Use with Lesson 8.

Name _____ Date _____

Safety Words

Vocabulary Reinforcement

The terms that go with each definition are scrambled. Unscramble the letters, and write the correct term on each line.

1. tysfea tleb • a strap that holds you safely in your seat _____

2. meelth • a head covering you wear to stay safe on a bike _____

3. fastey rage • clothing and equipment you wear to prevent injuries _____

4. saprenges • a person who rides in a car or other vehicle _____

5. stirf dia • emergency help that is given right away _____

6. ruinyj • hurt or damage to the body _____

Chapter 8 • Staying Safe
Use with Lesson 9.

Name _____ Date _____

A Trip to the Hospital

Reading Skills

Miguel's parents take him to the hospital. Put the things that happen to Miguel in the correct order. Write the letter of each thing that happens on the right line.

Things That Happen

1. First, _____
2. Next, _____
3. Then, _____
4. Then, _____
5. Finally, _____

a. doctors and nurses work with Miguel's family to help him.

b. the nurse checks Miguel and asks questions about how he feels.

c. Miguel rides out of the hospital in a wheelchair.

d. Miguel gets a name bracelet.

e. Miguel may have tests to find out what is wrong.

54 • Activity Book   Chapter 9 • Caring for My Neighborhood
Use with Lesson 1.

Name _____ Date _____

Vocabulary Reinforcement

Hospital Words

Color the puzzle pieces that contain an apple to find the vocabulary word. Then write what the word means on the lines below the puzzle.

1.

2.

Chapter 9 • Caring for My Neighborhood
Use with Lesson 2.

Name _____ Date _____

Recycling

Critical Thinking

Read the rules for recycling. Then sort the trash in the picture. Circle all the things that should be recycled.

Rules for Recycling

Our community will recycle
- glass bottles
- soft drink cans
- newspapers
- plastic jugs

Name _____ Date _____

Make Decisions About Trash

Life Skills

Each picture shows something that is usually thrown away. In each box, draw a way to reuse that thing.

1.

2.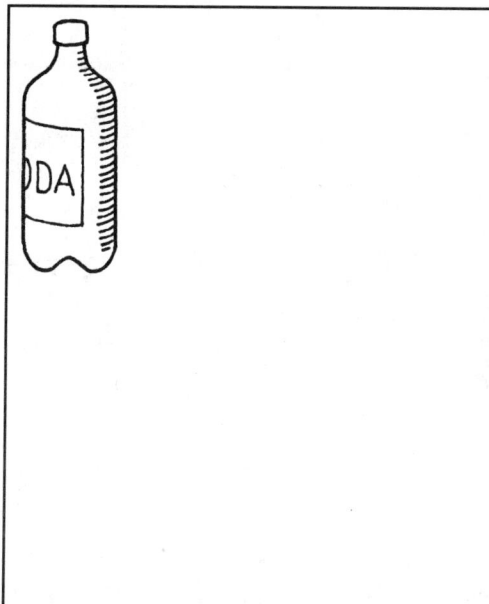

3.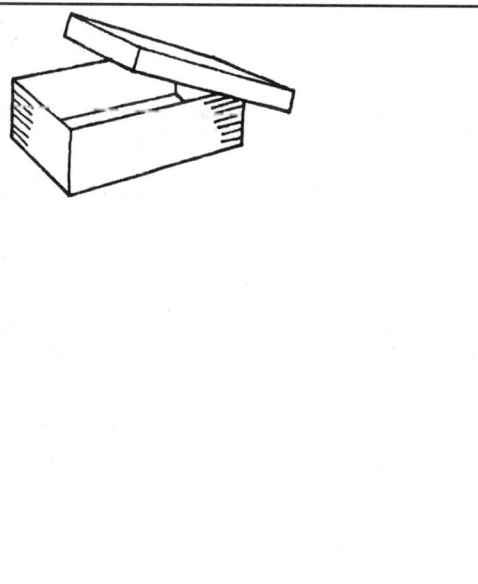

4.

Chapter 9 • Caring for My Neighborhood
Use with Life Skills: Make Decisions.

Name _____ Date _____

Facts About Water

Critical Thinking

Read each sentence. If the sentence is true, write **fact** on the line. If the sentence is not true, leave the line blank.

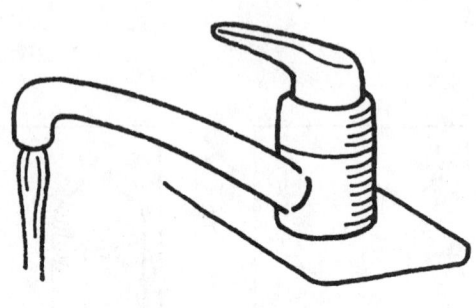

_____ 1. People need clean water to stay healthy.

_____ 2. Germs in water can harm people.

_____ 3. Animals and plants do not need clean water.

_____ 4. Community workers help keep water clean.

_____ 5. Some rivers have trash floating in them.

Name _____ Date _____

Land, Water, and Air

Vocabulary Reinforcement

For each definition, choose the correct term from the box. Write the letters of the term on the lines. The circled letters will spell what land, water, and air should be.

> air pollution
> recycling
> water pollution
> landfill

1. using things over and over instead of throwing them away

   __ __ (__) __ __ __ __ __ __

2. a hole in the ground that gets filled in with trash

   __ __ __ __ __ __ (__) __ __

3. harmful things in water

   __ __ (__) __ __

   __ __ __ __ __ __ __ __ __

4. dirt and other harmful things in the air

   (__) __ __

   __ __ __ __ __ __ __ __ (__)

Chapter 9 • Caring for My Neighborhood
Use with Lesson 6.